The Blue Tower

The Blue Tower

TOMAŽ ŠALAMUN

Translated from the Slovenian
by Michael Biggins with the author

HOUGHTON MIFFLIN HARCOURT
Boston   New York
2011

www.hmhbooks.com

Library of Congress Cataloging-in-Publication Data
Šalamun, Tomaž.
[Poems. English. Selections]
The blue tower / Šalamun, Tomaž ; translated from the Slovenian by
Michael Biggins with the author.
p. cm.
ISBN 978-0-547-36476-6
1. Šalamun, Tomaž — Translations into English. I. Biggins, Michael. II. Title.
PG1919.29.A5A2 2011
891.8'415 — dc22   2010049770

Book design by Melissa Lotfy

Printed in the United States of America
DOC 10 9 8 7 6 5 4 3 2 1

The Blue Tower was published in Slovenia as *Sinji stolp* (Ljubljana: Beletrina, 2007).

The following poems previously appeared elsewhere: *ABZ:* At Baroness Beatrice Monti
della Corte von Rezzori's. *Almost Island:* Marais; Pharaohs and Kings, Kassel, Paris;
Grischa's Fez; So We Don't Lose Our Virginity; Sounds Near Pistoletto; Diran Adebayo.
Bateau: Donnini; Title Still Pending; Florenza; Persia; Until Pessoa Nothing. *Descant:*
Marais; White Hash, Black Weed; Grischa's Fez. *Harvard Review:* Where Is the Little
Wall From. *Heat* (Australia): The Slave; Pleasure; Reminding Mankind of Yourself with a
Whip; So We Don't Lose Our Virginity. *New American Review:* La Torre, Celan; The Sirens;
San Juan de la Cruz Rolled in the Snow. *Nimrod:* Ptuj; Taverna. *North American Review:*
That's How Many Mighty Heaven Will Endure. *PEN America:* We Build a Barn and Read
Reader's Digest. Ploughshares: Honey and Holofernes; Trans-Siberia; San Pietro a Cascia
with Masaccio.

With thanks to
Baroness Beatrice Monti della Corte von Rezzori
and the Santa Maddalena Foundation,
where this book was written

CONTENTS

The Blue Tower

THE BRIDE WINS BOTH TIMES

To provoke the pasture's ladder, to wash out the cat's message,
What you hear through the walls is panic coming here.
In Morocco he whipped slaves. First I open the chest.
The ribs turn gray. I hold tight to the shovels, birds rip them from
my hands. I saw nomads, women on horseback. The dog days will
    come dressed in a
T-shirt. I'll show your hand, my hand is your hand.
Who drinks foliage through the silver of trees? A carriage couldn't
race by here, the brambles would wreck it. A believer
climbs the fence, look at that big little trumpet flaring its
nostrils. Debar clings to terraces, the house is full
of snails. Snow is beautiful. The moon calms his lips.
You flash him signals for cricket, eat chickens at midnight.
Isn't the wood for bramblebees rowing the river?
They think nothing of closing the eyebrows of someone like you.

GRISCHA'S FEZ

To chop up cotton and read through a cookbook.
To be running behind and hang from your lower jaw.
I'm free to drink bottoms up. Ganymede

gets stuck in a summerhouse. And oh how flowers grew by the
pathways. Do you see how I lopped off their heads?
Do you see how I step on his scalp as an officer?

They poured streams of hot water on me to harden my
mustache. They peeled the enamel off Cassandra's tooth.
By god, she marches over purple plums. She salutes and

keeps marching on the purple plums. A washed pot, if
you shine a deer in it, vomits craquelures back in your
mouth and eyes. King of the news, hitch up your sleigh, trample
the taffeta

and yarrow. There are petals in the cups. They beckon to a feast
of the moon. Elongated horses are the hairstyle around
the moon. Giants fight over cards. Giants rake

leaves. The rakes may go, the sand remains, the rakes
may go, the earth remains. Bang! goes a rake handle, and hits
a giant in the head, because somebody stepped on the

rake tines. Doves are the tiles between cathedrals. Woodsmen
bend down, get up, bend down, the town hall is split on its
peak. A peacock takes pity on a lake. Replace ✓

tooth with fake gemstone, woodsman with wooden
boat. Mists rampage in the comics. The horse is fond
of white. A beggar banging with a stick on the edge of

a bell has sand and rain pouring from his hat.
Gums are a cozy nest. Draw little jugs out of the clay. The Turks
made off with Srebrna while she drank at a well.

HONEY AND HOLOFERNES

I've invented a machine that, as soon as a goldfinch opens
its throat, starts dumping bags of concrete inside. Who licked the
    candies
into concrete, we don't know. Who then brought

the concrete to life, we don't know. The goldfinch sails. The goldfinch
sings. Where are you, Eugenijus? Racing across, opening
a hollow with your fingernails. You the pain of the contour, me

that of the train. Linda Bierds drives a car that comes
from the Tatras. The condor ripens the bird. My trousers smell like
gasoline. Do you see the pool? Do you see the pool? Do you see

the angel's elbow? It led me to those cliffs arrayed
like Vikings. Zebras have scraped eyes.
Ibrahim, Drago and Miklavž are great guys.

Iodine boils a bird's head. It dies in the mud. I
swallow bread. What did you see in the inner
darkness to earn it? A bifurcation for

both and the bent, silver-plated head of a
walking stick? Boxes of honey delivered
by parachute, which deer antlers

provided? Pythagoras is plunder. A cat licks
his ears all summer and winter. Pins directed
the bloodflow of saints. Stones erode

on the shoals. I shove Diran's head away from
the table. This clump is a tombolo. And that
pigeon on the plate. Mother of pearl. Gray head.

TRANS-SIBERIA

Every ball is a bloody, beautiful mask of powerful people.
We make up pretzels.
I always did like chickens.   .

O, slender fez, mildew perching on its fur.
The poet is an oafish celeb on a hood.
Of every wondrous power. On a hood.

I glance over my right shoulder and see
a lake with the canon bathing in it.
The marmots that shot past me weren't

marmots. Come on, god, sail off to abstraction.
Stepfather! Your mouthful eats soup, you only see it.
Nem Keckeget arrives in Japan and jumps down.

Us Us darns stockings. Here are the teeth of the
iron comb that still remembers the station
and steam, but for Cendrars no longer matters.

The only thing now is that you can't just
pleasantly say, "if you'd take off that shirt,
too," the way Marci and Hudi said it to me.

SAN PIETRO A CASCIA WITH MASACCIO

Radiant white pipe laughing deep down
in Jesus's eyes, the glow is astonished, returns. Wet
bandage wrapped around your head, does it hurt? Fra Angelico's
tongue is tin. The ants on it are the hills of
Tuscany. What was it that soaked Fra Angelico, nobody
before him had got so soaked. Lily pads grow out of the water.
Goat legs erase the copy. To flip, to stop, to drench
violence. To insert. To back up. To set down the toes, then the
heel. Not to look. To observe. To love the sun. Where is
the green from? Isn't the light from the windows? Fra Angelico had
suede shoes, a suede arm. A butterfly swimming from the blueness
    of the sky,
a flower doesn't tuck in its legs, only people
tuck in their legs. People sink into my heart
and are free. Fra Angelico spilled the bucket for us.

DIRAN ADEBAYO

Crete is valvoline. When the pony shuffled off.
I lie on a carpet. A German shepherd is a tulip.
Diran! A flower blooms for itself. You don't remind me

of him, you remind me of yourself. For Péru you point to a
bow for cricket and you pump, and pump, and rise. I am your
African lumpul. Diran! The earth has been trampled

here. Then Beatrice arrived. The sheep died
off. Their masters crawl into
dreams. Schloendorf has left. I've done my homework,

that vent, and now Laure, Péru and Juan
are the hosts here. Péru calls us outside to look at
the moon. Bella morena bianca. Enough to enrapture

the Nubians. A window, a traveler, a sail that drinks
up flashes. Kisses of light through the leaves of the trees, where
two birds are billing. A sweater lies dead across

the chain near the left headboard, that's wrong, near the white sheet,
that's right. You hear the birds sing, Diran,
you know that I've forgotten you. Hunters carry rifles

and stand up. Winter's coming. The rails will ice over
and those complaining now in their dreams — even
sheep trampled them — dissolve with a wave of a hand.

WE BUILD A BARN AND READ *READER'S DIGEST*

Quick ostrich. Quick ostrich. Quick sand. Quick sand.
Quick lime. Quick grass. The white juice from celeste Aïda,
and forgot-to-take-it dries up. The one

trampled by sheep (down below), Grischa and Beatrice
(up above) converse. They'd recognize each other in
a cover, a box, a jacket, a picture, in moss and trampled

dirt. At this angle of the sky
no pictures are allowed. Corpses are wrapped up like
sheaves. Dismiss the footprint. Wipe your eyes.

Stop pilfering. Grapeshot gets tangled up.
I go paying visits with my lives.
Here I just romped and touched the rug

with a yellow shoulder. I don't know what a word is.
To cry out *moth!* when on your white towel you see
a scorpion? El Alamein! Where is the difference?

Rommel was kissing heaven's dainty hands, and yet
from his airplane above the Sahara, my uncle
Rafko Perhauc still blew him to bits.

STRANGLING IN DREAMS

Via vaya, contolino.

The bench claps shut.

Canicula, canicula, my chest, my hat.

Canicula.

Masaccio was discovered in the next village over.

A bushel cuts the throat's angle.

It won't give me away.

Skull and crypt

Phallus — radish.

ALL THE INSTRUMENTS HAVE COLLAPSED

My bench goes to confirmation and hosts pistachios.

I remember Milenko wrapped in a toga.

Tearing out an accordion's guts means a lot.

Vanitas rotates the full moon smoking out of it.

Milenko preached at St. John the Divine, you don't

know if you can't see the cabin in the mirror. If you see yourself with

your fingers, wave. Stupica was finally ruined by his ambition

to paint a group portrait, a fresco, a monumental

work. Svetozar was in the chair at Dr. Rode's,

I waited outside with the fallen palate. I knocked

a cupboard out of the wall. I won, but nearly died. Barry

Watten told Miško Šuvakovič horrible things

about me. In my taxes a rabbit jumps

into the bull's eye of a cornea. Are you wet, white bird? What are

   you like?

WAITING ON ŠARANOVIČ STREET

Drawn moths don't penetrate the papers
or even get them wet. Goo-doo-lee, goo-doo-lah
rocks in my drinking cup. Death starts growing

in the sap. Short sticks fall in them. My grass,
frothy rouge, my grass, frothy rouge.
Flax intanats and then we're back at the velvet

munchkins. Knock on a door that's not there,
and the figs have red pits. Here's where the captain
with the dry skin swam. Exactly the same green

boot between the dark and the light Stradivarii.
When the Govic builds. When Cirila goes for milk.
I was father's driver. We rowed

like lightning. I wanted to be alone in the sand and
roll in it as the waves came. Lakes don't have any
plankton. Wire isn't wrapped inside the abdominal

cavity. It's an earthquake. Fruit touches the ground like
a lightbulb. The Ciudad floats on water and on the corner
a dog awaits me. Death is a ceramic. A Montesquiourous
　　　dog shits in it.

SO WE DON'T LOSE OUR VIRGINITY

Clay of silent diasporas, is water yellow
when the oar hits it flat? Where does
all the wool on the cliffs come from? Does the moon

send a compass? The color of feathers, of fur,
of skin and the heart's rumbling under volcanoes
all depend on the place where its point is

set in. The court imitates the river. Terry
had a sixty-foot-long tapeworm inside her.
That time the court won. We cut the tapeworm to pieces.

The pumpkin, the vessel, or more coarsely put, the body
was put together like a babushka — one cell
inside the other. The points of the seams smelled of

lemon. Then a hand began to stroke
the nipple. And side passages were opened
for the cavalries underground. That's how

we discovered the field of torches, which
began mating with sagas. There was no more Captain
Bada. Suddenly we had the word

anitra. The innocents made themselves a necklace.
And so we lived. Once again the cooking
was done by Cassandras, lovely

apelike monsters from the Carpathians. A horse
kissed me in vitro. Giudita offers me
her neck. I've stopped making eights with my bike.

WHERE IS THE LITTLE WALL FROM

The vehicle is simple. "Beauty sleep every day."
Eight kilometers from Lisbon by streetcar, going
west. Reader, escaping from my baskets, haven't you noticed? You
can't escape from five baskets at once. The baskets
shift like a juggler's balls. And we were off.
We walked and walked, naked, far into the militarized zone. Hey,
handsome! You're squinting beneath me. You have to look in my eyes.
You proclaim a new good and a tank drives into your mouth.
We didn't slam huts like these since little Friday's
times. You don't even have a proper terrace here. A duke or a horse.
Kerry sends me caravans of camels from the
furthermost parts of the world. My home is Persepolis.
I accept my gifts in a factory. I lived to see
Alexander. I kept Alexander alive.

STRANGE DREAMS

The Portuguese are bound with butchers and rampage
through the grass. Ubi, ubi, ubi, ubi, night? I carried
heaps of sand on the boat with a bucket. An otorhinolaryngologist
strengthens power. Let's drop this. I'll graze over
pastures. Listen to sounds in a bathtub. Aim my flashlight
at the stars. Up. At the treetops. Down. At the earth. Down.
At the ground. And zip, burrow my body into the air between cat
and bird. Between shotgun and stork. But the hunter doesn't
startle and shoots me above the waist, so my
lower part drops off, pants and all, and catches in
the bushes, waiting to be picked up and buried.
Silken lives end with "I wouldn't wish you a
splendid breakfast and a wretched supper," as
Professor Menaše warned me. God warns me with death.

AT BARONESS BEATRICE MONTI
DELLA CORTE VON REZZORI'S

An etching, a beautiful white etching, you're devoid of people,
devoid of bodies. What if we started flapping, or spinning like a
propeller, we would invite frogs and plums and sailors' earrings

so the air wouldn't be thin, or the place where we're going. Will there
be action? Will lightning flash? Will there be phantasms? Dropping
trees, just wires quickly twisted in a ball? Frank!

I eat you, after so long, after, let's say, Primož's
intermediation and what John says about where to plant the stakes.
John doesn't put it like that, those are my words,

John would like to come to Slovenia, but we are in
the buds, the fringe, the grass, the beech leaves, and I could ram
    Maximilian
Dorner into a beech trunk almost, look how pale

he is, you don't realize how much you've drunk, says Metka,
she always shows up and saves me, since I've had her I've been calm,
I have a home, nothing will blow me apart again, we'll die, for sure,

but all of us will die, that's the nicest part, when it's time of course,
not now, hey, the metaphors are all gone, metaphors are
the prow of a shipwreck, a swollen member, the dissemination

of Flemings, they really have come up, but where are we, I'm still
spinning that propeller, summoning the muse,
obviously, because in the night I got up and retyped

(saved to disk) what Peter and I had done. Paced
the rooms like a hawk and whispered, are you coming? are you?
I was a beast and snatched him from Tanya,

Tanya listens to Rufus, I also adore him, that time when I
drove Joshua to Lucca, we listened to him constantly, I
think we're off the ground, at least that's how my I perceives it,

here I am now, Beatrice, furious for having wasted
hours and hours with that third-rate professor,
a really overstuffed reputation, and hardly heard of

Grischa. Beatrice was the most beautiful woman of her
time and if I'd been hanging around Milan back then,
forget Tatjana, forget Nina, not even Monica Vitti, and

even she dried up, hanging onto Antonioni,
hey, there are no metaphors here, Jure would be pleased,
no he wouldn't, this would be too frivolous for him, we're left

where we are, we remain, we've had a nice life,
we have one. I saw a spider while I shaved,
le matin, le chagrin, I've got to get something out,

so that something is left for people if they call me up
today. How, the gifted ones constantly ask me,
how? Hey, Beatrice is bathing, I can hear the water splash.

"I DON'T LIKE PROUST, HE DIDN'T HAVE ENOUGH SEX," DIRAN SAYS

The mosque is a model of corporate shams,
Žiga shleps a hernia onto greenery.
I cattivi pluck hairs out of their nostrils, *perché*
i cattivi, perché non i buoni? I buoni e i
cattivi sono cattolici.
Sure, sure, Diran explains at dinner,
all the English boys at Oxford wanted
to sleep in my bed, and
we did, as innocent as puppies, but as soon as they grew their
first peach fuzz, my penis got bored and I changed orientation.
My mother prayed that I not catch the "English
disease." Nigeria is homophobic, and
you? It's late, it's late, my friend, and now it's too late.
Both of us are writers, neither one's a doctor, he also says.

PHARAOHS AND KINGS, KASSEL, PARIS

We had pretty girls and were excellent dancers,
Andro and I. The dual number is disappearing. We slid
over Karst mountains and drove to the sea. Do you remember
Cabiria? The skirts were long and people stared.
Everywhere people made way for you. But in Paris
at your Biennale des jeunes, it was *me* who prowled the night.
It's nice when young people cry with pleasure and you float and
listen to their sobbing. Robert became gay in the
sacristy, when a bear pounced on him. I reminded him
of that holy man. And who counts the souls that are
grateful to *him?* Tomaž Brejc said, what have you
been up to, you're so refreshed, and we're all rundown and
tired. It's true. I should have stood by Andraž back then
and trimmed his wings. Brothers can't sleep with each other.

TAVERNA

My bow of little rags doesn't symbolize
black ones. Bow of little rags?
"What do you mean by that?" Let's say a
lasso, let's say a net, that catches you and
makes you ask that question. As if you lit a smoke,
tunk, tunk, tunk, see how nicely it
burns. "That's cheap, dude,"
you don't need to invite anyone out to eat. Tak, tak,
yes, those are tiny little billfolds for communication.
A fishing pole for catching ones like you. Oops,
they fly off in the air and drop in the sea.
They smell of milk and of mother's gel
and when you grow up, you'll also be a famous writer.

BREAKFAST WITH MY HOSTESS IN ALDEBOROUGH

A pig went to a trough,
ate three silent birches, and that's supposed to be kind?
It is. It's how we summon the muse

on the farm. I eat the monkey's militias.
Kandahar is for appetite. In Moscow Vallejo
jumped into a fountain and burbled in the Neva, which he'd

brought to Moscow to honor himself for the occasion.
No water, no life. My husband was vice governor
of Hong Kong, that's why we're drawn there to this

day. And who's sitting at the table?
Chris Reid! That's right, Beletrina's slippers, here in
Aldeborough, just like the ones Peter has in Somerville,

they hide them from me in Slovenia.
I wander the world and put on your
slippers, did you plan this?

The lady's plan: to sail into St. Petersburg on her
yacht. She likes the way a city
opens itself to view from the sea. In Venice I met

Arne. He had also sailed into Venice with his
boat. I only saw mine once I'd
sold it and so managed to cling by my claws

above the abyss of poverty. My helpers in that
were Arne and both Japec brothers and here I declare
my gratitude, and let this all be recorded.

The boat's name was Nike and it was a sleek
Jeanneau. My kids have sailed in it several
times, knowing nothing about its owner.

SKATERS

I have no idea, some seventeen colors will
flood me, seventeen lego blocks of lime, shots.
Just listen and you see the smoke, you don't see the smoke,

the smoke is in your head (classic terra cotta)
the influence of my panna cotta for supper, I mean
you don't see the smoke, we've been here and I wanted

to mention the hunters, for lo their shooting (the Bible),
verily their shooting (the Bible) can be heard here
even now, while I type, and there really are too many, they

pop constantly, destroying the gentle creatures from Renaissance
pictures (disegno), while we, my I (unsettled)
go out, dividing up into beaters,

some of us following grandpa and then he fritters
it all (Brueghel), but back then I didn't know him,
what did I know, Ločje, Šentvid on Pesnica,

Ščavnica, the terrace that supported a bull and how
you weren't allowed to eat a single
grape if it wasn't served with a cup of water.

Where did all those fishponds go, they were flooded
for power plants and wigwams and ducks that swam around
the People's Park, all those clerics dining at

liberal tables (they got everything back, *doppio*),
and I've gone nowhere, slid no place, just that
lime that brought it up. Gundula stayed on the

surface, scarves flapped while we, whoosh, whoosh,
played on the frozen Rinza. That pheasant on Sovre's
table wasn't shot in winter. Never.

PRADA, MONTEVARCHI, BEFORE CÉZANNE

Plunge into the Drava, braggart. Your dainty gooselike fingers
will describe the arcs of living bodies falling from the bridge.
He crunches on the gravel. He swims and swims, can't swim across.
His shorts were torn off by a branch, he's bashful and won't get out here,
drowns. He swims and swims, can't swim across. Three paces
south with a pistol to his head. There is no decent water.
Heat eats his fiancée's breastbone. Greasy paper is left,
sausages, train cars. What sort of veil has been drawn across
you? What did Irina's two hundred dogs do in
Odessa? Where do you have your little fingers, on the buds or on the
canon? All it takes is for the strut to get worn and the
sail will burst. Death seems. It sags, hides
its spraying equipment, and beckons. Here I am,
great golden hen. I'm yours, great golden hen.

THAT'S HOW MANY MIGHTY HEAVEN WILL ENDURE

Janjica, Janjica, how do I get close to you?
How do I hear your bent paw? Tomatito plays
Spain. Pupae crawl onto people.
The angle is photographed from branches. Anne is coming
by train. Shall we go? Shall we go? Are the roads
crossed out? From the brooder to quiet workshops
where the clocks creak. Will the cypress fade? The coupon is *servus*.
Will the stone drink strychnine for people?
Why aren't you shaken? I lie in the bathtub
until after sunset one hundred stars
light up in the sky. Droplets of sweat that
drip down my arms in the sauna. Nothing. Slowly.
With a drawing. As many droplets as I
can endure, that's how many mankind will endure.

TITLE STILL PENDING

I palaksh around like a little Gypsy. I scrub three ribs
and get stuck. You'll scrub quite a few ribs
yet, just relax, with switches. With your eyes, with a fly, with leaves.
My complexion hums. A linden leaps into a new moon. It lifts up
    pamphlets.
The hollow ball of the earth falls to pieces. Whatever you water isn't
    drunk.
A panel board dewy head, leather head. Billions of pieces of
birds cast a spell. Will the shah absorb grain? Will
Robert Minhinnick ever publish Poetry of Wales?
Chamois will overgrow the transversal and freeze like a statue.
No one will be able to get past its fur.
Eyes come falling from the joints like some tiny
grape turds. Will lime ever comfort the
bristling wood? Brown, yellow, shoes with rubber. And at
the end, a haystack, a waterstack, Pont Mirabeau.

DONNINI

In San Pietro di Cascia.
To look at Masaccio.

In the butter of a huge linen hall
a hen kindles
Andersen's red shoe.

It thinks of brooding.
Be on my commanding hill and shut down my knitteries.
Let them keep watch. Let the tulip give meat.

Where did that sultan live, who lived near
the upper part of the red tulip's frayed
flag?

Bless you, cube.
If a unicorn stopped to the right,
the car couldn't get around it.

FLORENZA

Il gnoco. The upper dishwashing shift. Laure is sad
from the fluff. Juan moves around like a shadow.
Rocks dust Lipica. We fall with Ludwig's head.
Dry land. Sarah. I wake up in my T-shirt. They lifted
me up on a pulley, in silk. Do you sway when you slam
into the cliff walls? What does that do to your
bone prints? They put ointment on the little skins. Stored,
bound, cropped them. *Chiama mi.* I'll ride forth at
the fox hunt, from under the hide. Here's the spot where
Browning signed. I'm fond of Procacci. Pathway, pathway, *Bello
Sguardo. Ho mangiato il farro. Mi ha piaciuto
molto.* You, made of fresh moving body parts, the sun's
shining again. We folded up the buttonhole.
We gave, and gave, and gave, and gave, not there, and gave.

PERSIA

When I jumped on the sieve, the sieve
got sick. The word departed from the flesh and
became the fruit of Nicodemus. No one is free
of gentle bonds, buttons and ribbons
excepted. We dug them in pearlike flutters.
From there a short jump to a branch. Johnny Weissmuller,
such a well-stitched tarp, where do you see these now? We turned
gristle into myriads. Into mush. Into pharaohs.
Into Isfahan, where the square had no water. Into: let the
moon bang its knees or bang the stairs.
Do you hear how it's emptied enormous fields with chisels
and introduced acqua alta? Beatrice, Pascali,
Nono, speakers, wrapped in green and yellow, the
throat of the ship owner, where have I been that we've never met?

UNTIL PESSOA NOTHING

Leopard, droplet, leopard, why do you roll around
a lathe? Shiraz was the name of Pepi's cat. A violet
hoop, jostling in the whiteness if the sun drips,

thank you, if the rain drips, if it shines. Are killed
animals softer than unkilled ones? Covered with dirt,
what can you see? Lockets and octaves. An evergreen

spruce. A deep well and a shallow one, see how they
kiss. In-lining fox furs. Birds and flesh,
pierced with a wooden tip. You lick your lips

and ride on a lateral lift called an
iron horse. You put his hand in front of the lamp
to make figures. Bodies have feelers.

The roads are laid on a ventricle: mulatiera,
in the mountains, with windows, with steamships, Lilliput
is on water, tickles the earth's crust, protects it from

earthquakes. The steamships can vanish and continue
their way through the brambles. The fur
is bemittened. In oatmeal today, tomorrow in

an abyss. Now the squirrel already has teeth and a
compote of roof, bottom and sky. Horizontal
is for running and gathering. Horizontal

is for hoarding together food like
blankets heaped one on the other, to capture the
warmth. Camões sailed away by boat.

SCRUBBED SLAB, DARK SCREEN ,

What sort of icons? What sort of Rigas? What sort
of stelae? What sort of sheaf of trees? When does the oral cavity
consider where north is? When does it return
mittens? What comes between evaporation and
overheating? And what can we divide with a
tractor? The shooting of an arrow to its target? Can we
restore the gentleman who's sixty
feet tall, displaying his bones at
O'Hare? We travelers provided the slabs of flesh.
Memory is made of reeds. Handbags never
rot. Lakes leaning on your chest. Otters
like statues stowed before birth. Fine. Heels
in the sand, but I see. It started with Popeye and a
furious Olive Oyl. Persepolis was already washed by Disney.

A WORD TO THE HUNTERS

How the birdsong volleys!
I walk on a stroller.

"Selfish little beast, writing your own
stuff, who do you think you are?"

Calma, calma,
non sono un cinghiale,
don't shoot me.

THE TIP GROWS ON BEFORE THE STEP

The rudder is hungry.
A showcase fills up clocks.
A boy limps.
He's going home.

The wave waits.
Skin dresses
Billions of cross-joints, jackets,
ink pencils strewn like Russian fairy tales.

Brebis. My baby breviary.
Atalante's stroller of tinsel.
What are you up to like a wreck? The point is in the mineral.
This ant had a wrinkle on its wing.
I shut off the gas. The tree is in Brazil.

On a handsome yellow board that strokes the wing of a bird
up on a branch from below.
It makes an ellipse and bends left and right.
It forms a triangle.

Cut the boletus right under the hood.
Stay faithful to mites.
Mangle your hands.
Die them in a stork, so that
the golden gray gushes.

LA TORRE, CELAN

A ball a seascape, no man's Bogliasco, *il gruppetto.*
Lika cooks. Diran eats chickens on his own. Ahhh, floating
again, and I could care less whether there's algae below,

I spit in *l'abîme,* I spit in *the abyss.* I've gnawed through
the Question of Technology. It could have helped dead brother, since
they were friends, I dropped him at that point, stopped using

him at all, the one who threatened all Kakania from his Nazi
lectern, except you couldn't say that then,
I barely escaped from that snare, but

I do admire my dead brother, what would have saved him from
the Seine? Meat? Diran doesn't join in any meatless
meals, he can't stand salads. He touches himself. Not like in

Fellini, where the fat priest asks from the
confessional, *ti tocchi? ti tocchi ragazzo? ti
tocchi?* Diran circles around the table, scratching

his balls, but that entertains us, Alice is spoiled.
Tulips flutter in Dorset and in Turkey.
Anna is drawn to the plant. The botanical gardens have

all been closed in Italy, because art has devoured
nature. Taken all its money and not left a cent for
heating. It's been two months since Lika was last paid

and I've knocked over my modem. We're all paralyzed.
For three days Stefano has been calling for help, which
never comes. Albertina's in Milan. She's so pretty, and that's why

I jumped to kiss her as she left and got
tangled in the cords. Marco says he's calling us from
Riyadh, that he can't stand those Arabs. We know he's calling

from Milan and that he'd like to buy Beatrice's house
on Rhodes. Terry discovered black and white and red bugs
in the bathtub. Diran is afraid of snakes. His father beat him to a pulp

if he discovered him in London when he should have been in school
at Oxford. Diran is the biggest star on my horizon,
since Péru left and didn't ask me out to watch the stars.

THE SIRENS

I flower into shoulders.
Toss the snowball of a horse into the windberries.
Mildew. Chrysalis. A leg mouse scratches the slats.
Disappears and steps onto the deck of a typical boat.
Undoes the slats. Undoes the straps. Sunbathes its leg.
Watches the water splash and sunbathes.

Like a worm that gives its body away before it arrives —
where will he give it, at what points slice it up —
like a worm that gnaws, soaks up and hears cymbals.
Is that what a tail's for?
Do dolphins come and lead?
Do they bring wetness?
Which finally, flatly, bent over at ninety degrees,
waves in the snow before it departs.

IVO ŠTANDEKER

Soup, Rabelais.
Soup in your mouth.
A turtle in the soup in your mouth, Rabelais.

Come running, thief, come running, thief.
Dismantle the wall of sulfur barrels.
Dove in the vapor of my lungs,   ٭

lie down, close your eyes.
Get up.
Lie down and close your eyes.

AN HOUR

When the candelabrum started to lose its light,
they seized the chickens, everyone shook at the
thought of the coming winter. This winter is a snare.

This winter is a farcical knot. This winter sees a
threat in a wise guy. The next one will be
Galician. The bugs of next winter are already

staring, and if the curls get spoiled, then
Ropret will be out of his meals. It's a danger.
Honey is a joint over Jacob. He limps.

Professional soldiers get attacked by vermin
regardless of how many crumbs. To asphyxion.
To asphyxiation. Even she cheated her,

Anne-Marie Albiach. What is a pure
source and how does it smell. What did the flag say
when the head looked through it. Selim unrolls

a carpet for us to see. A mink. You walk on
black diamonds that attach
onto sleeves, that attach onto cuff links.

Fog is the hands of trees. It bends down and
opens the water. The thick hoarfrost hurts. A train
dunks it when it goes beneath the water.

An ibis extends its legs into a bonfire.
Do the kernels between the rings, in the places where
flesh is, flutter, hide, set up a

tent above them? I am conducted into an
arch. All of me is conducted. This is Uccello,
these are horses, these are horses' asses, banging

into a bead he can't sleep. When puff balls start to
crackle, when lightning starts to ooze, when the departing
open their flowers and the plant world starts to

drip water, that's when the gold of the gray reappears.
Cricket, cicada and mufti all step on the disk
and you, I, we are the first edges of stones

in a well in the woods. Tumbling through the air toward the
darkness comes pig, dolphin's godfather. Pig, dolphin's godfather?
My mother was a seamstress who kept forgetting

her cardboard. The equinox is a hawthorn. Tiles are ants,
soldiers step on each other's shoulders. Grown-up soldiers
spend the night outside. They sleep with their girlfriends.

Grown-up soldiers drink schnapps and make films of their
blisters. See how they stick to the tiles.
My ligaments got stuck to

Enver, who was Tito's brother. We miners use
our legs differently than proteuses do.
The fan won't exhale. It's held in hand by a

Japanese girl in Osteria dei Centopoveri.
Both of us eat duck with mushrooms. You go to the edge
and call out "Hepatitis! Hepatitis!" She comes,

thinking she'll get grain, and you
shove her over the edge like Cabiria. Winter
burbles. Opalescent refractions follow. Wonder, be

dumbstruck, Magellan, there are goose tracks in your
quiver. Hagia Sophia is a shutter. Milfoil should be
called fern. It's a horrible effort to tear off a

bandaid. Have you ever rooted an island out of the sea? Actually
heard the noise made by the water as it flies into the void?
Have you ever protected the mist with your own hand?

Legs spreading out like a peacock turn into glass
at the court. The sultan bestows them as copies for the heads
of tulips and for the crawl stroke in the harem pool.

SAN JUAN DE LA CRUZ ROLLED IN THE SNOW

I don't know if I'm Poltava, because I get attacked for nothing.
Go out to the black house and copy the clouds.
Take the cat with you.

We arrived at Tabor sunken in jugs of milk.
Before the war a marten used to dart around,
after the war a sign belched in your face.

The Danube isn't nubile.
The machine rumbles, the table shakes, the coffee squalls.
I moan like a statue that's had its beauty mark removed.

The curls are laid across the fire, I walk on
white embers. The girl on whose shoulders it will
fall draped hasn't yet settled in my awareness.

The slaves, prisoners in fact, evaporate on me.
They remind me of mother's flesh.
David has one hand too big.

Barbara Richter will give me a flat on
Uhlandstrasse. Diran told me yesterday that I have a
Stalinist zeal and that I'd like everyone

to believe in God. Terry also sees exactly that. Nuns
jumped from a great height onto his
bones. My curls have been cut.

RITES AND THE MEMBRANE

It sinks into movies, I sink into mortar.
Scythes and pincers of bugs are no homeland.
My questions burst the barrel, and a bullet flies out.

In the corners pits are put to sleep. The pool is covered.
The point of the pyramid over an urn, the stuccoed pyramid,
"Fat Joe, what's luv." The Jena is a river and the way you

warm your hands over the potbelly stove. I'm looking for chestnut
ice cream. These recumbent boards with huge wheels
race around the track for Icarus. Playthings, old pulleys,

so what is a waterfall called, if the waterfall's green,
a puzzle, a hand leaving its gesture, technology
melting sugar. Rice and bananas and eyes and a flower.

O taste of things, as I bent over in Limoges in the
twelfth century and worked on the Savior's little body.
I leapt over Grünewald and Pontormo, and kept throwing the wreath

off a viaduct. The white cat with the green ribbon wants me
to open the window. Even the steam was triumphal in the first
piston. Don't ever turn to follow a train. The earth gets

a lid to rinse off your soot. Most people
hold on to the strap. I think of the engineers
who set stone upon stone without even

touching it. The world is sprinkled with dew. The Soča
was installed. Its military bottom calls me, and there I'll shave
gnats. Before every lunch and after each birth.

SANTA RITA

Some grub worms feed me with an outsized spoon
and ask me if I can swallow all right.
A muff and a rag fly onto my head.

I dawdled under the window while
Kovačič was visiting Kocbek. Strip to the
waist and raise your elbows. Let's see

if your leg's going to jump. What do you see?
Spots? If it weren't for Glanz, I'd see
ice. They threatened to throw my dad in the Vrbas on account of

his pricey slippers. The road worker who rescued him got
an emerald, ask Andro, at one time I
said that he got a ring with a ruby.

On Durmitor the lungs can breathe. From Lovćen
you can see the sea. On Narlan's strips is written
"Lembranca do senhor do bonfim da Bahia,"

but he used to be my father. A knight on a
horse and a marionette. The chests all sank
and our enemies zipped through our throats.

Albertina's getting ready to dance. Her
voice is the voice of Živa Kraus. Her parents would put
carrots in her school lunchbox, instead of panini. Any instant I'll

ask galley slaves on board and invite them to row.
Chains and balls are a joke. Museums exhibit
boiling wine. How many plunks in the water

for every mile. How many potatoes
eaten, peels and all, to fend off scurvy.
I vote for the sound of rubber squeaking over

the sand. A flower stands still. The bison's a plow,
I've joined the adults who rang the bell. Who
went flying up with the rope. I lock up

the boat's oars, the attendant is gone. The one who puts
slippers on hooves has left for home. He's floating
down the river to a lake in Louisiana. Under the surface

he has a cabin with Catholic insignias.
The electricity flickers. Santa Rita is a martyr.
I have no idea what she did as a saint.

SOUNDS NEAR PISTOLETTO

The baker sang to them for four hours, ordered
catering and all those excellent wines, until he finally
dared to ask her about the scent that

Grischa used. I'm leaving for Cuba, because
I like the fellows there. Panini, panini, hills,
I never got close enough to see

the mosquitoes in the valley. Scrub and wood
were burning, I carried the hashish under my gums,
the dog won't smell you if I lick you all over.

Rinta, dove's rinta, when will you return
to your forests in Haiti? I saw you, and more than
once, the last time with Suzy. She isn't bashful.

I'm bashful. Suzy and John practically
belch on the same street. They're both bashful.
They've never met. I tell Zadie, you won't

believe, I'm holding a piece of paper
where Čander mentions you. The first time I heard
of you was when Beatrice introduced us.

Diran doesn't like her. They compete like two
mice. Diran is dancing to Fat Joe again.
Marie-Christine was jailed in St. Louis.

Fortunately they didn't stamp that in her
passport. At first I worked with young people, they're not
easy to put up with, her I met a long time ago, now I'm

a producer for Zeffirelli. Our forests in Haiti
are being cut down. I don't go there, it's dangerous, I'm an
only daughter, my mother described all of that in the

New York Times in August.
You don't know my mother and you say you saw
me. The two of us have been together for a whole

eternity. Paul is having Terry over, why don't you
come too. When I parked beneath that wall — out of 40,000
cars three go over every day, on average —

my car wasn't hit, my car got hit by a
kangaroo that was instantly killed. Me too,
man, when I finally smuggled the hash under my

gums (in Singapore they hang you, that made it
more exciting) and got it nice and ready before
breakfast, I always use it to celebrate when

I get to someplace new and I add the country's name
for the benefit of philistines, since even philistines
are part of democracy and etiquette. Only the prince-bishop
        commands

where to sow cabbage. Bodies jutting out, bugs
rasping, water running short and the pen is black.
Nature is beaten down into a concave gloss.

Because my father didn't lash any Jews, I'm
protected. Whiteness from a dark cup. Coffee
from a quiet street. Frescoes have a smell. The head

is Sirah's body. For three centuries we've been living
off matches. I chain a kleptomaniac to a
pear. The chain can't slip off because the

pear gets fat toward the bottom. I invented a pane
with three cantons and used a periscope like Živko.
I'll bet not just the picture from Marezige, I'll bet

you even have my Lujo statue in your cellar. What will you do
when the hunter's horn starts poking its way through your
soul? What will you do when you find out Snežnik isn't

yours anymore? What will you do when you encounter a bear,
grumbling, looking around for a pair of slippers. Take them off
    so they don't
give you blisters. Lower your periscope. And the canoe, the falls,

the kayak, all those rubber deals, so you bounce gently,
pull in your knees, pull in your knees, Živko!
of course I'll shove into your Postojna

Cave through a quiver. Putin learned from me
to poison before a hand even touches the trigger.
Diran doesn't have his black belt and I'm not

forbidden to say his name. I prize human
beings. In the clay they're lovable creatures. In Venice
I fell in love twice: with a fifteen-year-old girl in a

fur, on the Ponte dell'Accademia, and with a
seventeen-year-old boy who constantly
put on and took off his sweater in front of me at the Bacon

retrospective. All the attainable ones, wings of a dove,
I've brought along with me. Dunk the
veil. Made out of fox lairs, sleeps

blissful dreams. The horse climbs up on four
legs. I leave my driver. I leave my bike.
The joints pale and go rusty. Honor beats the bags.

THE GENTLEMAN IS A BIT INCLINED TO DISORDER

What I softened and what I didn't soften
what I stabbed into Ogrizek's body, they say
he had a dog that ate bones. I warm myself,

close the armoire, turn off the light in the
bathroom. Yesterday I steamed like a horse after
riding. O scents of stable manure, o spurs

of Dr. Ewa Rogalska's late sister, *Pan jest troszeczkę
nieporządnym,* Christine told me, because she'd been
told to say that to me, instead of preparing

the servants properly for welcoming a guest.
Servants have to have a plan. They can't help it if they've
forgotten history. Servants have to be

ready for blows from the most unpredictable
quarters. Masaccio draws a red piglet in the middle
of the church, and this is what I told him: I'll pay

for everything but your whores, that would cross her, and I
don't like anything to cross her, or what I told
Andraž. Go and saddle up. In Sejno they'll

teach you to ride at least well enough for you
to talk about it. You've been silent long enough.
Out of that Dostoyevsky cage of yours. Žižek ran off. Only

Jani Razpotnik came with me. Žižek hid around a
corner, I clearly remember. They had just
made those holes beneath our house, Ravnikar wants Bologna,

the machines clattered away beneath my bed and they moved
Mrs. Novak out, while Žižek hides from me behind the
wall where Miška is now. Besides, *il n'a pas bien roulé ses*

r, but Jani could. We insisted that the director of the
French Cultural Center deal with us, and
not with so-called French cultural

interests. Just where do you think you've opened your
center, we told him. And left. It turned out
Žižek was more cunning. He hit them straight in the

heart and buttered up that Milner, that
worm who forced his way into the party line till
Slavoj liquidated him. Now and then he still spits at me,

but less and less. Andro has stopped riding. *Pan jest*
troszeczkę nieporzą-dnym just as much and Janko simply thinks
(I'd got on some stairs beneath an eave, since it was

raining and Janko with his shining face asked: what are you doing
up there on those steps — he was convinced I'd gone
mad, and that he'd find some relief — hey, Janko, it's

raining) and Šumi, who turned me like a screw,
spoiled brat! — of course those weren't the words he used —
young man, for years and years I was Stele's gofer, I'm giving

you the directorship after all. What Župančič? Izidor
Cankar! Oh, no, I said, Župančič even so.
He kissed ass once or twice, but you resent that

just because you kissed some ass yourself. Who cares! *Chi se ne
frega!* That multitudes in hoods and bonnets came out to
sing him serenades, and that as a child I stood before

his bier and in my mind's eye closed his eyes again, drew the
lids down like a pair of shutters, was only fair. He was a
clever one, too. He knew his grandson and I would be

al pari one day and he wanted to protect him. Nice try.
I'm here to detonate your incest, so that now
his, others' and my gentle snow can fall on you.

MARAIS

I dreamed that Martinique was reheeled with water.
La bouche, la bouche, André kept repeating, when
Andraž and I lived in Sing Sing. Did I chase him
because his name was so close? I told him
how I'd endured Senghor, that boats came floating from heaven,
falling on Lake Ohrid like fairy flies, that we
danced with our nephews, great-nieces and bodyguards,
all the ones that were here to keep them from staging a coup there.
　　His locals
lured me to a monastery. Okudzhava wore black
shoes. I was the sweet party elite, sweeter than your
mouth. Palms flutter in Senegal. The priests wear cassocks.
And once, as I walked back from the St. Paul metro station, after
Semolič and I had been drinking at George's, I was picked up
by the same guy who had caught me at the words *la bouche, la bouche.*

LINDOS

Thirty police cubes heaped up on an open
head. The syllabus: geoglyphs in Nazco. Set fire
to the wrapper wall of a one-year-old snake that has pimples
(vents) on the inside of its line. Icarus
hid his feathers under some fig trees. They lifted
me up in a basket. Little donkeys are handy.
They sleep on porcelain, covered with quilt.
A coil of heaven, blueprint of the mouth. What do chimneys
support, as they smoke from the belly? Who is
the outer circumference of a baker? In summer cold
clay is enough. And a lapidarium in the next country over, chopped
straight into the water. Mirrors are the defense of
pure little bug legs. The Greek god has a scythe on
his windlass. See how the boat crawls now.

WHITE HASH, BLACK WEED

Gregor tells us what you're up to.

There's humor tucked away in the chalk of the white spots.
People ask me how I get my eyelids to
sink. It's simple: skin,

stroke a dolphin, sometimes set Armenia on fire.
Diran knows exactly. Hash helps, hash is a
walker. Not for him, he's black, for him it's

weed. Marco called again. He
really means to buy Lindos. And I think about
Juan (his mother-in-law, the psychiatrist,

who trained with Lacan, frustrated because
there are no real customers in Naples), sure he checks out
when he thinks about the Nazco lines. Mostly they've

left to gather mushrooms, and I'm alone.
I'm riding yesterday's weed and even Diran's
typing. He's in the tower. He's got everything

poured into his computer. But me, if I'm not
physically chopping wood, I get lazy. My cornea is eaten
by torches, and dwarves in togas come rolling out of

geoglyphs. It hums, and if anyone has ever really thought how
to build a house, it's Juan. In Pittsburgh they also want
me for a semester. Liliana Ursu wants me

to write her a foreword. "I'm hot in
Kuala Lumpur." Quite well known in
Singapore. Only to a precious few in

Jakarta, but they're on fire. In Jakarta
people don't have much money and have to
borrow my books. I still have that sheet,

Andrej, that you gave me on the flight to
Asia. All packed away. I'm not making things up
and not lying. Not exaggerating. Except

when I admire Marco's boat.
It's hopeless. It eats up so much gas.
No wonder you can't sell it

to anyone but a Saudi prince
at a loss, maybe the one who
cruised me on the Greek islands.

He designed and tracked it down himself. You
track down an invention like a hunting dog. And we were
melancholy everywhere. I've actually chased

Archilochus. GLADSTONE WAS A
PIG. I ONLY LIKED DISRAELI,
I hear distinctly. Just as Pogorelić

got everything from Liszt, via living people,
so now can I drink deeply from
the English crown. That has strategic

significance. Marco Canoni. Look it up.
O your eyes, Queen Victoria. O your
white feathers. But young dots do

the same. They're on the dense, on the tiny and
the fresh. I'm on the rare, the horrible and
mad. But not sold out. Not sold out.

I'm fighting with Primož's prediction that
I'll end as gilding, that I'm just playing.
Deit strokes my head. Deit has a say in the catch.

THE SLAVE

A slave placates my godfather. The left sleeve is
too short. I'm with you. Root out every
half-splinter half-straw from the base of the

brush. I'm with you.
O grain, forming a sphere from your stalk.
Destroying and building churches.

Bending a clapper.
Spitting on crumbs pressed into the sand by a horse
hoof.

Why did you land here and not there?
How deep do you sink?
A screw would be no fun, you saw and

shoved off. The noises are fairy tales. So are the foams.
The light
turns around. A bird flickers like lightning and

sings like lightning.
Copying its divine gift.
The last sap of the beams in a trench, before it pays its caste.

I'm charming. I've subjugated.
I discover some change in my
hand.

A berry falls onto a drop.

Ardent la belle, where are you?

I've retreated into the cream inside the bread.

I hear the paws of Teddy, the black dog, as they

echo off the grass as off a carpet.

He also loves and desires attention.

LIME TREE

Dane was handed around by Parisian counts
who offered him trips on their yachts around Africa.
And now me: would you go with me to Kuala

Lumpur? "Who will get it?" A pear is stuffed
with a piano, o exvalidated. The surrealists kept
everything under glass. Their piano lay alone

amidst clouds resembling some Tyrolean fence.
A pear stuffed with a piano, o exvalidated,
accomplishes three times thirty thousand times as much

as the queen bee in her hive. When Beatrice buys and samples
cheese (it's true, Tonino, the serotonin in pecorino, with ruccola
and chianti make you dream towards morning

that you've lost your keys, your wallet, and all your
cards) people are stunned. She takes a fig, gives it
first to me to bite a little off, then tries it

herself, and puts whatever's left back into the grocer's
hand. People learn. Even in Tuscany they've forgotten
quite a bit. They're only now

discovering why Masaccio was tremendo,
why he struck Gentile da Fabriano to the quick
when still a boy, not to mention (but which

Longhi said, long ago, though no one believed him)
what he did for Fra Angelico. He made Fra Angelico
ready for God. Till then he'd painted cliffs like

Bosch, little monks like Bosch, and his animals
carry something in their mouths like one-headed
stars. I open the corridor. There are people

gathering in it now, who'd also like to get bread,
while the two of us just try some, turn it,
cold-bloodedly preparing ourselves for slow food.

The people get that instinctively, although they
had those idiotic Savoys instead of
proper noble souls. And Pan opening

Radovljica is worth six hundred silks. Rock me,
Vintgar, little paw. There it's blue, there it's
cool. There an old man sits on the cliffs, eyes bulging, like some

haggard eagle. And there I, the sun, retreated early
and left you in peace to develop. You can also
feel free to forget those five hundred postcards. A leg

cut into a pine doesn't bleed like a leg snagged on a
cork tree. Rabbit carries his lettuce and house
on his back all by himself. And Bloom really is

fat and really does look like Bloom.
Terry stroked him while he lectured about the
Mormons. Yesterday she was a lizard, a canicula, a

cassiopeia, because I can't spit straight out what she
really was — an iguana. Diran and I danced ourselves
bloody at the sight of it. I'm sixty years old.

My soul is growing. I scare Metka by gurgling as I
wake up. By wheezing like a volcano. When I move
my body like a mountain to my studio, these little

rabbits jump out of it, before I've even
finished washing up and exercising. Those spiritualized worms
spring up if I wander the world.

FLIGHT

Vesper sketched bird, glossolalia.

Do you remember? From out of those little cheeks and boxes

at Novi Sad Radio?

I've been bound to the nipples with sticks.

Ouch, Bermuda mattress!

Ouch, Bermuda mattress!

A strong bird that extricates itself to winter,

planning a rumba for part of the sky.

It materializes as flying geese.

I went to the movies to sprinkle myself.

Conscience stings the coffee, rolls out a dead pie.

Hairpins go flying from wall to wall,

as do Turks, bearing three mythical titles:

Commodore of the Turkish Opera. President of the Chamber

of Turkish Architects. But we're not there.

We're here: the young archbishop of Constance has a Jacuzzi.

Lorraine under a blotter. O my herbarium.

Tannin and a rolled-up bag, where are epic elements?

Six broad-shouldered, six men.

It wasn't till Delaware (when we missed the exit) that I sensed

how dew is produced on the skin of America.

What if I wrapped all these pieces up in a kerchief and numbered them.

I religiously take off my slippers and put on a shoe.

I religiously listen to the sounds in my body.

I will religiously open the door and go out to smoke.

PTUJ

Refuse from a tundula.

The caro anita of mankind.

These are lions on a bridge without manes.

Stampless horses without bellies.

Pupolotti (bulbs) that burn out and get changed.

A real bridge with a real foundation, with real water, and a wet
shadow. What here can be walked across, we always swam.

Spinning our hats and stovepipes in the seawater.

Fashion doesn't grow old. Water doesn't grow old.

The turning point in the nest should be overpaid.

I remember you with knitting needles in your lap, when you used them
to point at Rafko.

A buck loped down from the castle.

Rosette, a rose, Rosika. Where Mazlu, Stančič

Avšič, Mrs. Abramič, and Mrs. Senčar (née Ban) gathered.

First wipe off the knife, then the grave.

The soldiers are marching off to sleep.

SUGAR ·

Hidden in the kraut-and-bean soup and amidst numbers was the tarp
   (the *cerada*)
for covering people's fates. We were rigging the boat
when a new order came. Everyone onto the truck with the people's
fates, we'll cover them, if we must, with our bodies.
It was one of those frequent scenes when you install
seats in trucks, because you want people to be comfortable.
Houses were burning. The cork had been stinged. Blood flowed
down the sinkhole to the sumac and soaked into the earth.
Now doves and ants take turns scratching it out.
Depending on whether it's ovaltine or rice. A Red Ant, hidden
behind some backpacks, didn't know that we'd sliced up his tent.
What to do with the flag. What to do with a glass chicken.
Boccalin appears in poems. The grownups sing our theme songs.
   All morning
I fling my pot around the boat deck and watch people.

ATHOS

The stump was wrong. Hermelin dies as soon as I open my eyes.

We painted the fish pull-on,

and it jutted down.

It wagged its tail in the water, in the Greek mountain.

There were flies on the roosters,

the flies were the first to open their throats.

Athos sun, Athos lava, and the looks from people.

Fish wagged their tails under the sea

we saw from here.

Armoire lava, armoire lava,

we've included the faithful.

The abandoned and debased.

Cut into a pear so the blood ran.

Giacometti's cart was on the bench.

Its posts shone blue.

Elijah's chariot was between my sleeve and fur lining.

I cast a spell on a little monk.

He got up like a count. He got up like a son. He got up like a swordsman.

If I lean on my shoulder, the forest hums.

LETTER FROM KEVIN HOLDEN

TIGER TIGER TIGER TIGER TIGER

There are tigers everywhere

Dream tigers, paper tigers, tigers in trees, in snow, in my tongue &
stars

Dear YOU

In the Blue Tower   .

Please tell me if you receive this
At this address

I have been thinking of you

Thank you for the Postcard
Yes!
Les Rois!

I was away over break — In New York
Art
Brooklyn
& With my mother in Rhode Island
The SEA
I walk around
Like a TURTLE

& The Pines
& Elsewhere

So when I returned, I had it
Planet, CATHEDRAL

I miss you

I had a dream about you
Sledding & the Snow & Wolves
They were friends
A cave of Winds

The poets speak of you
You are loved here
When do you come to the United States?

Here is something (else) with which I am in love:

"Art is at present the only construction complete unto itself, about
which nothing more can be said, such is its richness, vitality, sense,
wisdom. Understanding, seeing. Describing a flower: relative poetry
more or less paper flower. Seeing.

"Until the intimate vibrations of the final cell of a brain-god-
mathematics are discovered along with the explanation of primary
astronomies, that is the essence, impossibility will always be
described with the logical elements of perpetual contradiction, that
swamp of stars and of useless bells. Toads of cold lanterns, squashed
flat against the descriptive intelligence of a red belly. What is written

on art is an educative work and in that sense it has a right to exist.
We want to make men realize afresh that the one unique fraternity
exists in the moment of intensity when beauty and life itself are
concentrated on the height of a wire rising toward a flash of light, a
blue trembling linked to the earth by our magnetic gazes covering
the peaks with snow. The miracle."

Tzara

Isn't it wonderful?

We should go find Tristan in the Trees & love him

Distribution center
The hollow
The birches

Tell me news

Here there is snow!

Tiger
Dreams

LOVE

THE FLIGHT INTO THE LAND OF EGYPT

A cypress that sets up camp at home base and licks the eyes of the
    egg king.
Of an elephant that distinguishes wheat flour from rye.
The one that climbs up a ladder, then spits capers down.
A catfish with its eyelashes yanked out.
The one who lifts a rock and moves the rock.
The one who draws in the sand the precise route for the invasion of
    Egypt.
Sovre, in person, alone, drinking black coffee on white lace,
setting the black coffee down in its white cup next to the pheasant.
Honey and trout and capers and berries.
It has started to rain now in Thebes, for only the second time in
    Thebes's life.
I have discovered a tin watering can.

Alice washed herself off into me.
If the railroad helped the ball, then the ball buried the railroad.
No! The wall straightens out. The fur coats are stunned.
Diran bends down over Nanni's ear, Beatrice takes pictures.
No! Don't take the jacket, go around the cutlet.
Are you here?
I am.
What are you doing?
Crunching and drinking water from the porters' fountain.
Only the stewed fruit is traced.

The nature of the impoverished is in the earrings, where white
   cypresses grow.
Red, glowing eyes that get stuck on the railings of bridges.
So do you protect them with silken nets?
"What should be flat?" The surface?
The grass where you bounced la balle before stepping into the bite?

The chakras pour out October.
I fall on a body and see a chanterelle, or rather I wonder
if you can already see three hours after sunrise.

What really soaks a policewoman's kuglo, what really scrubs her
   sleeves?
Cash and a heart with flour and suds drive through the reeds.
The fine carpet is of ice, here's where the catfish and fortresses pass.
Fragments of castles gurgle forth out of gold-iced, formed bast.
My ear. My home. Intention?
Give me the ermine bird, one eye green, one eye crimson.
Half of the guards sleep leaning.
From eyes to eyes you dip the plant, from eyes to eyes.
What will you assemble out of the kite, dying Murn?

A gullet slithers up the mountains.
We bathe ourselves.
We won't trample the songbird in our galoshes and ponchos.
Faruk offered a prayer ticket.
Faruk has left the land of Egypt.
Back then I had a cabbie's hair.
We had lunches and dinners at Jošt's.

We have each other.

Horse, pissing on my forearm and biceps,

on my blue and black line tattoo.

What did it cost Persia to lay pipes into Asia.

La Sua Eccellenza Governatore Generale del Canada,

these days the finches regulate the weather in Asia.

In Canada the sun drops way down in the evenings.

What hurts comes to the light of day on its own.

THE SOUL MURDERS THE TILE   ·

The soul murders the tile, shoots it to bits.
Nicholson translates air with desire.
I translate a face with a hut.
A ball with a broad lap,
an incantation with coffee, a block with a subway.
A flag with a cap, a cap, your pith cap.
The night with soil.

Those of you who come will vanish, and those of you who vanish will
    come.
Young, lazy and too slack to cut my throat, as
Caravaggio did, because I was a zero to him, less than a fly that
disturbed him. Go find Shakespeare! Obsessed with himself,
and my doors burn and shine around his soul.   ·

I was the first to hurl a stone from the tower of Babel.
I was the first to blink.
I was the first to slaughter my mother and a servant, then
cleanse and purify myself.
To lie on the grass like fresh laundered linen.
The first to ride through the blue woods on a deer.   ·

And yesterday evening, as Alice — Beatrice's favorite dog —
made love to Diran, both of them have horrible, red tongues, thorns to
the living. A white oar to my soul.
I, the silverware under the angle, chief of the unreasoning,

a stone,

smoke that sleeps through its scent, I give

the Prater to my spades. I don't smell them anymore beneath my

angle.

In the cold, thin air I eat locusts and am a saint.

Here's the beginning of my crown.

The spheres on its tentacles bark and lick in the boats.

We're lost in a jungle where we

bear on our shoulders the physics for Christ's body.

At Rodez Artaud wore an apron.

My bones meet their ends in the ether, on the anvil.

Dove of the hungry. Thread of the mortal. Astrakhan of multitudes.

Dad.

BROTHER

The little arms are commanding. Wet, they steal the canister.
The molten lead that flies through my body forms a
flower. I kiss the baker on the mouth. I'm here.

A bulb of bright-colored, blue ones, a bison's butterfly,
a fang that snuffs out its prey and then rolls up into a
higher, squeaking body. You turn the soul over,

you eat the steak. You breathe and the nylon squeaks.
It ruts, crunches, rides and cleans itself in a cupboard,
the one that brought me here in a box, at first in a

box. Checking the king's balls. He brings the
drug. Why shouldn't we nail the tongue to an
arch? Two tongues. Two symmetries. And we'll

scrape them with the blade of a scissors so that they curl
(bend up) like the ends of a ribbon that are left free
when you wrap up chocolates and flowers. So that Celan

might swim in the Seine. So he might do the crawl through the
    Tuileries,
as I did. Beneath every tree they lay, covered
with trinkets and tape left from parcels marked

UNRRA. The sound of the tape. A sled in the snow.
A sled in the snow. A sled in the snow, a mountain of dark ones,
a mountain of bright ones. My tree is the incantation.

PLEASURE

What does bleaching mean, brilliantined
pug,
black heart with a red tongue.
Whom did you make love to on the couch and then set the couch on fire?
The tower ignited, the tower was almost blown to bits,
tiny bits of the gommapiuma burned down.
Alice predicted
the flame with her red tongue and you predicted
the flame with your red tongue.
It happened on the ninth of October, 2002,
from half a million to a million people marched
peacefully, and Terry was moved
to tears. Albertina danced a flamenco and opened the
belino and then came the fire.

THE BLISTER

Soy in earthen pots, a Roman.
Koper sticks its fly in my pillow, the flowers are lovely,
the bees are lovely, lovely blood, lovely blood,

the fire is lovely, the smells rising from it,
a flood brings grayness and cold, everything's clean.
When a blister comes out of the body, does it thirst?

It's wet, it crackles, together with Bruno and Saint
Francis, with Halal, the bruises that Saint
Stephen gets, some stones bounce off,

some land softly, others hit and he screams,
here, here is your home, drive out my heart,
egotistical factory consuming chairs like a boa,

It gives chanterelles to Venuses, the weather has bounced off.
So what if its wings spread enough to drain swamps,
black mud sucks down its trunk. From the leaves, parts of frogs,

frog eyes and the moss on trees rolls something
like a carpet, its scales showing silver.
They become the brother of north or south, which calls,

they start to flutter. Sometimes it digs out
a well. Pops out. Air gurgles in the throat of the
earth, and we in the sky. Boatsmen have often

explained that our own sand covers the mind from the light.
Sirens are crackle, snap, pan-fried dough made of flour and
pears. Some get their skin flayed, others their eye

sockets moved, two thirds of Tuscans were
cashiered near Florence. But the olive trees
bore olives again and puppies, peacocks and beautiful

caterpillars picked them until people recovered just
enough for their little arms to reach up.
Oil from the olives drove off the plague. Red tongues

just faked fire. If a heavy iron ball
drops from a great height onto his bones,
crunch, the swelling, the stalk, it all belongs to the river.

REMINDING MANKIND OF YOURSELF WITH A WHIP

What do you swing your club and spew pits for,
Thousand and One Nights?
I gaped at the frescoes.   ·

Who would have thought they were so scribbled over.
The paint has peeled off.
The walls are heavy and wide.

I divide Africa along its head, so we'll all be warm.
The loaf hits the platter sliced, just
a bit sliced.

Blueberries, strawberries, an appetite, shutters.
Set down your sleeves, set down your sleeves, set down
your class, the foam around your mouth.

Do you recall the pilgrims on Ptuj Hill that
Mihelič painted, the candies you devoured
and the little vinyl Boy Scout blackboards?

Manure smells of nobility, not a stable.
My pages are all over the place, with
ants walking on them.

Today is June 28, Saint Vitus's Day. What have we postmarked?
Babies carry kindling.
A pelican fans warm embers up to its waist,

so that our anthem can crash more dramatically on the rocks
of the Adriatic. Nabokov doesn't recall this,
he came here later.

I want up on the gallows.
I'm approached by a gentleman who
also wants up on the gallows.

I've been approached by ladies who had the most beautiful
hands in this or that city.
When did I miss my descent?

CHIUNQUE GIUNGE LE MANI

Tar of hoplites
Timava, turn round
on a pram, at a car, at a fence
the famished door of the sun, rain
savages clean up after themselves
Vikrče in a wigwam, out, five fingers, one missing
five fingers, sticky titmice,
missing FARO

light

mommy's cramped spaces

no bookworm, no bookish vase
test tubes behind gilt doors
ropes, pikes
whispering buona sera
ranks bounce, a hunting dog
iodine, iodine, iodine, the bellet gets pitchy
it runs like an animal-god, a train-bird
probability preserved
a hail of departed
dandelion dodge

terrine, timeo take off
disheveled hair
ree gee dee vee dee mo
a bow to the cricket sky

tug tug tug

kate sacking off

december sip sip sip

howls into a magnetic heart
che devono fare
spin threads
teach olive trees
bits of the next day in john the fireman
resoled auras

june bug has countless coats

sesame to the prince of the door
to hack out a verb with a tschor polenta
you live on the tiny grass
you live and don't hack out verbs
live birth the arm rots

winged well-drained bessarabians
came to the house
lifted the silt
i stand in for happiness

                  age of pleistocenestimated seed

an expanded creature
supple water lily, crotch of beanpole
the living are fine with a corpse
a clod in a granite flute's studio
venus, bright goldfinch

Donnini, autumn 2002